AMERICA'S
LOST
WARS

AUSTIN BAAS

America's Lost Wars!

Austin Baas

Published by Austin Baas, 2023.

Table of Contents

DEDICATION

To the countless souls whose lives were swept away in the tides of forgotten wars, this book is dedicated to you. In the hallowed echoes of history, where the narratives often overlook the sacrifices made on the obscure battlefields, we extend our heartfelt tribute to the millions who bore the weight of conflict's heavy toll. Your stories, though lost in the pages of time, remain etched in the collective memory of a nation. May this work serve as a humble homage to the resilience, courage, and sacrifice of those whose footsteps tread the paths less remembered. In honoring your memory, we strive to ensure that the sacrifices of the past are never truly lost, but rather serve as poignant reminders of the human cost of war.

ACKNOWLEDGMENTS

In the pursuit of unraveling the threads of history, this work stands as a testament to the enduring spirit of those who have graced these pages with their stories, their struggles, and their sacrifice. To the countless individuals who, in the course of America's forgotten wars, became unsung heroes and heroines—your legacy lives on in the pages of this book. We extend our deepest gratitude to the families and communities whose lives have been indelibly marked by the profound impact of war. This endeavor would not have been possible without the dedication of historians, archivists, and researchers who tirelessly seek to preserve the intricate tapestry of our past. To the veterans who generously shared their experiences, and to the memories of those who are no longer with us, we express our sincere appreciation. This work stands as a collective effort, a mosaic woven with the threads of countless lives, and we offer our heartfelt acknowledgment to all those who have contributed to the illumination of history's often overlooked chapters.

1.

Unearthing America's Lost Wars

In the vast expanse of history, there exists a trove of untold stories, concealed beneath the well-known narratives that have shaped our understanding of the American experience. Like layers of dust settling on forgotten manuscripts, the annals of the nation harbor chapters obscured by time, waiting to be uncovered and brought into the light.

This book is an expedition into the uncharted territories of America's past, a journey that seeks to reveal the clandestine, the overlooked, and the obscured. For within the broader tapestry of the nation's history lie threads of conflict that have quietly woven themselves into the fabric of our identity. It's an exploration that transcends the familiar battles etched into textbooks, inviting readers to delve into the concealed recesses where the true depth of our history resides.

In the symphony of America's narrative, we often hear the crescendos—the thunderous clashes of revolution, the echoes of civil strife, and the resounding booms of world wars. However, it is the subtle notes, the whispers of forgotten conflicts, that add nuance to this symphony. This book endeavors to amplify those whispers, to unmask the stories obscured by the passage of time.

As we embark on this literary excavation, envision it as a journey of revelation and rediscovery. Each chapter is a step deeper into the recesses of our collective memory, where we unearth tales of bravery, sacrifice, and resilience that have long eluded our awareness. It is an odyssey that aims to redefine our perception of history, revealing the hidden landscapes that have shaped the nation we know today.

So, dear reader, join us as we lift the veil on the undiscovered, unfurl the maps of forgotten campaigns, and illuminate the obscured corners of the American story. In the simplicity of words and the elegance of revelation, this book invites you to witness the unfolding of the untold—a literary voyage into the heart of a nation, unmasking its hidden chapters of war.

2.

Wars Before 'Independence'

In the quiet corridors of history, before the thunderous roar of cannons and the signing of the Declaration of Independence, the American landscape bore witness to a series of forgotten conflicts—a prelude to the birth of a nation. These early struggles, often overshadowed by the Revolutionary War, were the quiet murmurs that echoed through the vast expanse of the continent, shaping the destiny of a people on the brink of transformation.

Clash of Cultures: Indigenous Wars and Colonial Intricacies

Long before the notion of a united nation took root, the American continent was a tapestry of diverse cultures, each with its own intricate history. The clashes between indigenous nations and European colonists were not merely battles for territory; they were complex interactions marked by alliances, cultural exchanges, and tensions that would lay the foundation for the turbulent centuries to come.

As European settlers ventured further into the unknown, encounters with indigenous peoples became inevitable. The resulting conflicts were not only struggles for land and resources but collisions of vastly different ways of life. Understanding these early colonial conflicts unveils the nuanced stories of survival, adaptation, and resistance that marked the meeting of two worlds.

Border Skirmishes: Prelude to Revolutionary Fervor

The frontier of early America was a fluid and contested space, where colonists and Native Americans grappled for control. These border skirmishes, often relegated to the periphery of historical narratives, were the crucible in which the seeds of resistance were sown. Long before the rallying cries of independence, there were localized conflicts that fueled a sense of shared identity among the colonists and set the stage for a larger struggle against imperial rule.

These were not just battles for land but moments of profound importance, where ordinary people asserted their autonomy and began to envision a future free from external control. The forgotten battles on the periphery were, in essence, the rehearsal for the grand drama of revolution.

Unheralded Sacrifices: The Overlooked Patriots

Amidst the well-known figures of the Revolutionary War, there existed a legion of unsung heroes—individuals whose sacrifices paved the way for the eventual quest for independence. These were the unheralded patriots who, long before the revolutionary fervor reached its peak, dedicated themselves to the cause of liberty.

Their stories may have faded into the background, but their contributions were instrumental. Whether through acts of defiance, resilience in the face of adversity, or tireless advocacy for the principles that would define a nation, these overlooked patriots played a vital role in laying the groundwork for the larger struggle that lay ahead.

Forgotten Alliances: Colonial Wars on the Global Stage

The early conflicts in North America were not isolated affairs; they were part of a broader canvas of global imperial rivalries. Wars between European powers spilled over onto the American continent, shaping the destinies of colonies far from the theaters of European conflict. These forgotten alliances and conflicts, often overshadowed by the larger narratives of empire, had a profound impact on the trajectory of the American colonies.

Understanding these global dimensions provides a more comprehensive view of the forces at play during this era. The early struggles in America were not isolated; they were interconnected threads in the intricate web of global geopolitics.

As we reflect on the wars before independence, let us not merely view them as distant echoes of the past but as vibrant chapters that enrich our understanding of the complex tapestry of American history. The clash of cultures, border skirmishes, unheralded sacrifices, and global entanglements were all part of the intricate dance that led to the birth of a nation. In revisiting these early struggles, we gain a deeper appreciation for the resilience, diversity, and indomitable spirit that shaped the United States in its formative years.

3.

The Indian Wars: Clash of Cultures

In the annals of American history, the saga of the Indian Wars stands as a poignant chapter marked by the collision of two worlds. The story of America seems very similar to the story of Palestine, which was later colonized by Europeans. Long before the birth of the United States, the vast expanse of North America was a tapestry of indigenous cultures, each with its own rich history and traditions. The Indian Wars, a complex series of conflicts spanning centuries, encapsulate a profound clash of cultures, a struggle for land, resources, and a way of life.

The Tapestry of Indigenous Nations

Before the arrival of European settlers, the continent was inhabited by diverse and thriving indigenous nations. From the Algonquian peoples in the East to the Navajo in the Southwest, each community had distinct languages, customs, and spiritual beliefs that shaped their way of life. The clash of cultures that ensued was not merely a military confrontation but a clash of worldviews, values, and ways of understanding the land.

European Encroachment: The Seeds of Conflict

As European settlers established colonies along the eastern seaboard, the expansion westward brought them into direct contact with established indigenous societies. The clash was inevitable as different notions of land ownership and land use collided. European settlers, driven by the idea of private property, sought to impose a system of ownership that stood in stark contrast to the communal and spiritual connection indigenous peoples had with the land.

From Trade to Tensions: The Fur Trade Era

The fur trade, initially a source of economic exchange between Native American tribes and European traders, became a source of tension as demand for pelts grew. The fur trade era saw the introduction of firearms, changing the dynamics of intertribal conflicts and intensifying competition for resources. What began as a mutually beneficial economic relationship transformed into a catalyst for conflict.

Land Cessions and Broken Promises

The United States' westward expansion brought forth a relentless push for land, leading to a series of treaties and agreements with indigenous nations. However, these treaties were often marred by broken promises, deceit, and a fundamental misunderstanding of indigenous governance systems. The forced removal of Native American communities from their ancestral lands, such as the Trail of Tears, remains a painful reminder of the deep scars left by the clash of cultures.

Military Campaigns and Resistance

The Indian Wars, a series of conflicts that unfolded across different regions and time periods, saw both indigenous resistance and military campaigns by the U.S. government. Notable battles such as the Battle of Little Bighorn and the Wounded Knee Massacre reflect the complexities of a conflict rooted in differing perspectives on land, sovereignty, and the future of America.

Legacy and Reconciliation

The Indian Wars cast a long shadow over the history of the United States, leaving a legacy that extends into the present day. The clash of cultures during this period has left indelible marks on the social, economic, and political landscapes of the nation. Today, the ongoing efforts towards reconciliation, acknowledgment of historical injustices, and the revitalization of indigenous cultures are steps towards healing the wounds inflicted by centuries of conflict.

In revisiting the Indian Wars, we confront the uncomfortable truths of America's past—a past marked by a clash of cultures, broken promises, and a struggle for survival. Understanding this chapter in history is not only a testament to the resilience of indigenous peoples but a crucial step in fostering a more inclusive and equitable future. The clash of cultures during the Indian Wars is a reminder that the intricate tapestry of America's history is woven with threads of both triumphs and tragedies.

4.

The Quasi-War: America's Undeclared Naval Conflict

In the closing years of the 18th century, against the backdrop of the French Revolution and the rise of Napoleonic France, the fledgling United States found itself entangled in a conflict that would come to be known as the Quasi-War. Unfolding largely at sea and often overlooked in the expansive tapestry of American history, the Quasi-War was a unique chapter marked by naval clashes, diplomatic tensions, and a delicate balancing act between war and peace.

Backdrop of Political Turmoil: The French Revolution and Its Impact

The late 18th century was a period of political upheaval in Europe, with the French Revolution sending shockwaves across the Atlantic. As France descended into revolution, the United States, with a fragile economy and nascent government, found itself caught in the crossfire of European power struggles. The Franco-American alliance forged during the Revolutionary War now faced challenges as France sought American support in its conflict with Britain.

Undeclared Hostilities: The Genesis of the Quasi-War

Amidst this geopolitical turmoil, tensions escalated between the United States and France. The signing of Jay's Treaty with Britain, which was viewed unfavorably by the French, and the XYZ Affair—an embarrassing diplomatic incident involving French intermediaries demanding bribes from American diplomats—marked a turning point. In response, President John Adams faced a difficult decision: to go to war or to pursue a different course of action.

Naval Engagements: Conflict on the High Seas

The Quasi-War, although undeclared, manifested primarily in naval engagements between American and French vessels. Privateers and warships from both sides clashed in the Caribbean and the Atlantic, with notable figures like Thomas Truxtun and Stephen Decatur making their mark during this tumultuous period. These naval encounters were critical in shaping public opinion and influencing the diplomatic path chosen by the United States.

Diplomacy Prevails: The End of the Quasi-War

Despite the naval confrontations, the Adams administration prioritized diplomacy over all-out war. The signing of the Convention of 1800, also known as the Treaty of Mortefontaine, marked the end of the Quasi-War. The resolution, negotiated by American diplomats including William Vans Murray and Oliver Ellsworth, brought an end to the hostilities between the United States and France, reaffirming peace and normalizing relations.

Legacy and Lessons: The Quasi-War in Historical Context

The Quasi-War, though brief and often overshadowed by the more monumental conflicts in American history, left a lasting legacy. It showcased the challenges a young nation faced in navigating the treacherous waters of international relations. The diplomatic resolution emphasized the value of negotiation and dialogue even in times of heightened tension, setting a precedent for future conflicts.

In the context of the Quasi-War, the United States demonstrated a commitment to avoiding unnecessary military entanglements and prioritizing diplomatic solutions. This pragmatic approach not only preserved the nation's stability during a tumultuous period but also contributed to the shaping of a diplomatic legacy that endures today. The

Quasi-War, with its naval clashes and diplomatic resolutions, remains a testament to the complexities of early American foreign relations and the delicate dance between war and peace on the international stage.

5.

War of 1812: The Second
War for Independence

In the pages of American history, the War of 1812 is often referred to as the "Second War for Independence," a conflict that pitted the United States against Britain once again. However, the perspective of this war takes on a unique and often overlooked dimension when seen through the eyes of the indigenous peoples who inhabited the lands caught in the crossfire. For Native American nations, the War of 1812 was not only a struggle for independence but a battle for the preservation of their ancestral homelands, cultures, and ways of life.

Treaties and Broken Promises: Precursors to Conflict

Before the outbreak of the War of 1812, indigenous nations had already experienced the encroachment of European settlers and the erosion of their lands through a series of treaties. Many tribes, including the Shawnee, Creek, and Tecumseh's pan-Indian confederation, were deeply affected by the steady encroachment of American settlers onto their territories. The promises made in treaties, often rendered obsolete as the nation expanded, left a trail of broken assurances that fueled indigenous grievances.

Tecumseh's Vision: A Pan-Indian Confederation

Tecumseh, a Shawnee leader, emerged as a central figure in the indigenous response to encroachment. His vision of a united front against American expansionism sought to forge a pan-Indian

13

confederation that transcended tribal boundaries. The War of 1812 provided an opportunity to realize this vision, as Tecumseh allied with the British in hopes of stemming the westward tide of American settlement.

The Battle of Tippecanoe: Prelude to War

The Battle of Tippecanoe in 1811 marked a significant moment in the lead-up to the War of 1812. Tecumseh's confederation clashed with American forces led by William Henry Harrison, resulting in a costly defeat for the indigenous alliance. Despite the setback, the conflict foreshadowed the broader struggles that would unfold during the War of 1812, as indigenous nations grappled with the expanding reach of the United States.

Indigenous Allies and Adversaries: Navigating Alliances

Throughout the War of 1812, indigenous nations faced complex choices regarding alliances. Some, like Tecumseh's confederation and the Creek Nation, aligned with the British in the hope of securing support against American expansion. Others, such as the Choctaw and Chickasaw, sided with the United States, seeking to protect their interests in a rapidly changing landscape. These alliances, forged in the crucible of war, had lasting repercussions for indigenous communities.

Aftermath and Consequences: The Toll on Indigenous Peoples

The Treaty of Ghent in 1814 formally ended the War of 1812, yet the consequences for indigenous nations were profound and enduring. The conflict did not halt the westward expansion, and the post-war era witnessed an acceleration of settler encroachment, leading to the further dispossession of indigenous lands.

Legacy and Resilience: The Indigenous Perspective

For indigenous peoples, the War of 1812 left a legacy of displacement, broken treaties, and profound change. The struggle for independence, as seen through their eyes, was not solely about the geopolitical dynamics between the United States and Britain but a fight for the survival of diverse cultures and the preservation of ancestral homelands. Despite the challenges and losses, indigenous communities displayed remarkable resilience, adapting to new realities while maintaining their distinct identities.

As we revisit the War of 1812, it is essential to acknowledge the multifaceted narrative that unfolded during this period—a narrative where indigenous nations were central actors with their own aspirations, challenges, and sacrifices. The War of 1812, viewed through the lens of indigenous perspectives, offers a richer and more nuanced understanding of a pivotal moment in American history.

6.

Mexican-American War: Manifest Destiny and Its Costs

In the mid-19th century, the United States embarked on a contentious and expansionist chapter known as the Mexican-American War. Fueled by the doctrine of Manifest Destiny—a belief in the divine right to expand across the continent—this conflict reshaped borders and left an indelible mark on both nations involved. Yet, beneath the grand narrative of territorial acquisition, the Mexican-American War exacted a toll, with profound costs and consequences for those caught in its tumultuous wake.

Manifest Destiny Unleashed: The Ideological Underpinning

Manifest Destiny, a prevailing ideology of the era, asserted that the United States was destined to expand its dominion across North America. This fervent belief fueled westward migration and justified the acquisition of new territories, regardless of the consequences for the indigenous peoples or neighboring nations. As tensions simmered between the United States and Mexico over disputed territories, Manifest Destiny provided a moral justification for territorial aggrandizement.

The Spark: Texas Annexation and Border Disputes

The annexation of Texas in 1845 ignited the powder keg of long-standing tensions between Mexico and the United States. Mexico viewed Texas as part of its territory, while the U.S. saw its annexation as a fulfillment of Manifest Destiny. Border disputes and conflicting claims over the Rio Grande or Nueces River as the boundary further escalated the brewing conflict, setting the stage for war.

War Erupts: Battles and Campaigns

In 1846, hostilities erupted into open warfare. The conflict saw key battles, including the Siege of Fort Texas, the Battle of Monterrey, and the pivotal Battle of Buena Vista. American forces, led by figures like General Zachary Taylor and later General Winfield Scott, faced Mexican defenders in a war characterized by both conventional military engagements and guerrilla warfare.

The Treaty of Guadalupe Hidalgo: Costs and Consequences

The war concluded in 1848 with the signing of the Treaty of Guadalupe Hidalgo. This treaty, while ceding vast territories to the United States—including California, New Mexico, Arizona, Nevada, Utah, and parts of Colorado, Wyoming, Kansas, and Oklahoma—brought about a complex legacy. The cost for Mexico was staggering, resulting in the loss of over half its territory. For the United States, the acquisition of these territories inflamed sectional tensions over the extension of slavery.

Human Costs: Impact on Indigenous Peoples and Mexican Citizens

Amid the geopolitical maneuvering and territorial exchanges, the human costs of the Mexican-American War were profound. Indigenous peoples inhabiting the contested regions faced displacement, violence, and cultural disruption. Mexican citizens, caught in the throes of war, endured the hardships of occupation, battles on their soil, and the social upheaval that followed the signing of the Treaty of Guadalupe Hidalgo.

Legacy and Reflection: Reckoning with Consequences

The Mexican-American War left an enduring legacy, shaping the trajectory of both nations involved. The acquisition of vast territories fueled the expansion of the United States, but it also laid bare the ethical and moral quandaries inherent in Manifest Destiny. The war's consequences reverberated through American history, contributing to debates over slavery, sectionalism, and the nation's role on the global stage.

As we reflect on the Mexican-American War, it is imperative to recognize its costs—the lives disrupted, territories reshaped, and the complex legacies inherited. Manifest Destiny, once embraced as a noble pursuit, carries within it the shadows of a turbulent era. Understanding the human toll and consequences of this conflict prompts a deeper examination of the narratives surrounding westward expansion and forces us to confront the complexities of America's past.

7.

Civil War Redux: The Forgotten Battles of Reconstruction

As the smoke cleared and the echoes of the Civil War faded into history, a new chapter unfolded on the scarred landscape of the American South—Reconstruction. While the Civil War was officially over, the struggle for the soul of a nation persisted in what can be described as a Civil War Redux. Beyond the familiar battles etched into the collective memory, a series of forgotten conflicts emerged during the tumultuous era of Reconstruction, each a poignant chapter in the unfinished saga of post-war America.

1. Battle of Liberty Place: Reasserting White Supremacy

In 1874, the Battle of Liberty Place erupted in New Orleans, Louisiana—an event often overlooked in the broader narrative of Reconstruction. Fueled by racial animosity and resentment towards the political changes imposed by Reconstruction policies, a coalition of white supremacists sought to overthrow the biracial government in the city. The battle marked a violent attempt to reverse the gains made by African Americans during Reconstruction and restore white political dominance.

2. Colfax Massacre: Bloodshed in the Quest for Political Power

The Colfax Massacre of 1873 stands as one of the bloodiest episodes during the Reconstruction era. The dispute over the outcome of a local election in Colfax, Louisiana, escalated into a violent clash between white supremacists and African American Republicans. The massacre, which claimed the lives of over a hundred African Americans, highlighted the ruthless tactics employed by those opposed to the political and social advancements of Black citizens.

3. Hamburg Massacre: Struggle for Black Political Representation

In 1876, the small town of Hamburg, South Carolina, became the battleground for a clash between armed Black militia and white supremacists. The conflict arose from tensions over the appointment of a Black militia captain, part of the broader struggle for political representation and autonomy for African Americans in the post-war South. The Hamburg Massacre underscored the challenges faced by Black communities seeking to assert their rights in the face of entrenched white resistance.

4. Battle of Fort Pillow: Tragedy in the Aftermath of War

In 1864, the Battle of Fort Pillow in Tennessee unfolded as a grim reminder of the racial animosity that persisted even in the waning days of the Civil War. Confederate forces, led by General Nathan Bedford Forrest, overran the Union-held fort defended by both white and Black soldiers. The aftermath of the battle saw the massacre of surrendering Black troops, highlighting the racial tensions that would continue to plague the South during Reconstruction.

5. Coushatta Massacre: Suppression of Republican Influence

In 1874, the Coushatta Massacre unfolded in Red River Parish, Louisiana, as part of a broader effort to suppress Republican influence and intimidate those aligned with Reconstruction policies. The massacre targeted white and Black Republicans, including elected officials, revealing the lengths to which opponents of Reconstruction were willing to go to reestablish political and social hierarchies.

Legacy and Reflection: Unveiling Hidden Chapters

The forgotten battles of Reconstruction, marked by political upheaval, racial violence, and struggles for power, represent a complex and often overlooked period in American history. While the official end of the Civil War brought hopes of a united and reconciled nation, the battles waged during Reconstruction laid bare the deeply entrenched divisions and the arduous journey toward true equality.

As we delve into these forgotten conflicts, we uncover a tapestry of resistance, resilience, and, at times, tragedy. These battles, though overshadowed by the grandeur of the Civil War, are integral to understanding the unfinished nature of America's post-war transformation. The legacy of Reconstruction, with its triumphs and tribulations, continues to echo through the corridors of time, reminding us that the struggle for a more perfect union is an ongoing and multifaceted endeavor.

8.

The Philippine-American War: Imperial Ambitions Unveiled

As the 19th century drew to a close, the United States found itself thrust onto the world stage, driven by newfound imperial ambitions. The Spanish-American War of 1898, ostensibly fought to liberate Cuba from Spanish rule, marked the beginning of America's foray into global affairs. However, what followed in the Philippine archipelago revealed a darker side of imperial aspirations and the clash between liberation and subjugation.

1. Treaty of Paris and the Fate of the Philippines

The Treaty of Paris in 1898 officially ended the Spanish-American War, resulting in the cession of several territories, including the Philippines, from Spain to the United States. However, the aspirations of Filipino nationalists for independence collided with American desires for imperial expansion. What began as a war against colonial oppression soon morphed into a new conflict as the Filipinos found themselves in the crosshairs of their erstwhile liberators.

2. First Battle of Manila and the Shift in Alliances

The initial stages of the Philippine-American War saw Filipino insurgents, led by Emilio Aguinaldo, assisting American forces in defeating the Spanish. However, as aspirations for Philippine independence clashed with American imperial designs, the alliance fractured. The First Battle of Manila in 1899 marked a turning point, signaling the shift from a supposed partnership to an open conflict between former allies.

3. Guerrilla Warfare: Filipino Resistance

The ensuing Philippine-American War was characterized by a protracted and brutal guerrilla conflict. Filipino insurgents, employing hit-and-run tactics and leveraging knowledge of the terrain, resisted American occupation. The conflict, marked by atrocities on both sides, revealed the high cost of imperial ambitions and the resilience of a people fighting for their right to self-determination.

4. Balangiga Massacre and Retaliation

One of the darkest chapters of the war was the Balangiga Massacre in 1901. Filipino insurgents launched a surprise attack on American troops in the town of Balangiga, resulting in heavy casualties. In retaliation, American forces, under the command of General Jacob H. Smith, ordered a brutal counteroffensive. The town was subjected to a scorched-earth policy, with the infamous order to turn the island of Samar into a "howling wilderness."

5. Brutal Counterinsurgency: Water Cure and Concentration Camps

The American military's response to Filipino resistance was marked by brutal counterinsurgency tactics. The use of "water cure," a form of torture involving forced ingestion of water until the victim vomited, and the establishment of concentration camps to control civilian populations underscored the harsh measures taken to suppress resistance. These methods, later condemned and investigated, left an indelible stain on the reputation of American forces.

Legacy and Reflection: Unintended Consequences of Empire

The Philippine-American War, often overshadowed by the concurrent events of the Spanish-American War and the subsequent Philippine independence movement, holds enduring significance. It laid bare the contradictions within American ideals of liberty and self-determination, revealing the complexities of imperial pursuits. The unintended consequences of empire-building in the Philippines would resonate for decades, shaping the course of American foreign policy and influencing global perceptions of U.S. intentions.

As we reflect on the Philippine-American War, it serves as a stark reminder that the pursuit of imperial ambitions comes at a profound human cost. The clash between liberation and subjugation in the Philippines unraveled the ideals professed by a nation that had itself fought for independence just a century earlier. The scars left by this conflict continue to echo in the Philippines' national memory, prompting a nuanced examination of the price paid for imperial ambitions and the enduring struggle for genuine self-determination.

9.

Banana Wars: America's Intervention in Latin America

In the early 20th century, a series of conflicts and interventions unfolded in Latin America, driven by economic interests, political instability, and the strategic importance of the Panama Canal. Dubbed the "Banana Wars," these interventions marked a period of significant U.S. involvement in the affairs of several Latin American nations, leaving a lasting impact on the region's political landscape and shaping perceptions of American foreign policy.

1. Economic Interests: The Rise of United Fruit Company

The origins of the Banana Wars can be traced to the economic interests of powerful American corporations, most notably the United Fruit Company. These companies, seeking control over banana plantations, railways, and ports in countries like Honduras, Guatemala, and Colombia, wielded tremendous influence over local economies and politics. The term "Banana Republic" was coined to describe nations where the economic and political structures were heavily influenced by foreign fruit companies.

2. Political Instability and U.S. Interventions

The early 20th century witnessed political upheavals and instability in several Latin American nations. In response to perceived threats to American interests, the U.S. government intervened militarily in countries such as Nicaragua, Honduras, and the Dominican Republic. The interventions were often justified as efforts to restore order, protect American lives and property, and promote stability, but they frequently served to safeguard the interests of American corporations.

3. Occupation of Nicaragua: The Chamorro-Bryan Treaty

The U.S. intervention in Nicaragua was marked by the occupation of the country from 1912 to 1933. The Chamorro-Bryan Treaty, signed in 1914, granted the United States the right to intervene militarily in Nicaragua to protect American interests. This interventionist approach aimed at maintaining political stability for the benefit of American corporations and securing control over the strategically significant Nicaraguan canal route.

4. United States in Honduras: Caudillos and Interventions

Honduras, another focal point of the Banana Wars, experienced a series of interventions during the early 20th century. The U.S. government intervened to protect its economic interests and support friendly leaders, often referred to as caudillos, who would align with American policies. These interventions, while ostensibly aimed at preserving stability, left a legacy of political interference and resentment.

5. The Occupation of the Dominican Republic: Stability and Control

The U.S. occupation of the Dominican Republic from 1916 to 1924 was another significant chapter of the Banana Wars. The intervention aimed to restore political and economic stability, ensuring the repayment of foreign debts and protecting American business interests. While it succeeded in bringing a degree of order, the occupation left a legacy of anti-American sentiment and a perception of the Dominican Republic as a client state.

Legacy and Reflection: Consequences of Intervention

The Banana Wars, despite their short-term objectives of maintaining stability and protecting economic interests, had profound and enduring consequences. The interventions fostered anti-American sentiments, contributed to the consolidation of authoritarian regimes, and fueled a perception of the United States as an interventionist power in Latin America. The legacy of the Banana Wars looms large in the collective memory of nations affected, shaping diplomatic relations and influencing regional dynamics for decades to come.

As we reflect on the Banana Wars, it becomes evident that the interventionist policies pursued in the pursuit of economic interests left a lasting impact on the political landscape of Latin America. The tensions between sovereignty and foreign influence, as manifested during this period, continue to shape the complex relationship between the United States and its southern neighbors.

10.

The Siberian Intervention: America's Forgotten Expedition

Amidst the tumult of the Russian Revolution and the ensuing Russian Civil War, an often-overlooked chapter in American military history unfolded—the Siberian Intervention. From 1918 to 1920, the United States, alongside other Allied nations, intervened in Siberia, sending troops to support the White Russian forces against the Bolshevik Red Army. This forgotten expedition, marked by complexity and ambiguity, sheds light on a period when the world grappled with the consequences of revolution and the uncertainties of post-World War I geopolitics.

1. Context of Revolution: The Russian Civil War Unfolds

The Siberian Intervention took place against the backdrop of the Russian Revolution of 1917, which led to the overthrow of the Provisional Government and the rise of Bolshevik rule under Vladimir Lenin. The ensuing Russian Civil War pitted the Red Army (Bolsheviks) against the White Army (anti-Bolshevik forces), resulting in a complex and multifaceted conflict.

2. Allies in Siberia: Objectives and Ambiguities

The Allies, including the United States, Japan, and European powers, intervened in Siberia for a variety of reasons. Some sought to protect war materiel sent to the Eastern Front during World War I, while others aimed to prevent the spread of Bolshevism. The objectives, however, were often ambiguous and varied among the participating nations, leading to a lack of cohesion in the intervention effort.

3. American Expeditionary Forces: The Polar Bear Expedition

The United States, part of the broader Allied intervention, deployed troops to Siberia as part of the American Expeditionary Forces. The most well-known contingent was the "Polar Bear Expedition," comprising U.S. Army forces. These American troops found themselves embroiled in the complexities of the Russian Civil War, facing the challenges of harsh Siberian winters and a shifting political landscape.

4. Japanese Presence and Tensions

The Siberian Intervention witnessed a significant Japanese presence, with Japanese forces occupying parts of Siberia, particularly in the Russian Far East. Tensions among the Allies, including the United States, Japan, and other European powers, added complexity to the intervention. The differing objectives and rivalries among the Allies underscored the challenges of conducting a coordinated military operation.

5. Legacy and Ambiguities: Unanswered Questions

The Siberian Intervention, although largely forgotten in the annals of American history, left a complex legacy. The expedition's objectives were never clearly defined, and the American troops found themselves entangled in the intricacies of a foreign civil war. The lack of a decisive impact on the course of the Russian Civil War and the ambiguity surrounding the intervention's goals have contributed to its status as a little-known episode in U.S. military history.

Reflection: Unraveling the Threads of History

As we unravel the threads of the Siberian Intervention, it becomes clear that this forgotten expedition reflects the uncertainties and complexities of an era marked by revolutionary upheavals and geopolitical realignments. The intervention, driven by a mix of motivations and fraught with ambiguities, invites us to reexamine the role of the United States in the global landscape during a period of profound transformation. The Siberian Intervention, with its unanswered questions and historical enigma, stands as a testament to the intricate dance of nations navigating the aftermath of revolution and the uncertainties of a new world order.

11.

The Korean War: The "Forgotten War" Revisited

In the shadow of World War II's colossal conflict, another war unfolded on the Korean Peninsula that would come to be known as the "Forgotten War." From 1950 to 1953, the Korean War left an indelible mark on the geopolitical landscape, shaping the division of Korea and influencing the dynamics of the Cold War. As we revisit this oft-overlooked chapter in history, we unravel the complexities, conflicts, and enduring repercussions of the Korean War.

1. The Division of Korea: Seeds of Conflict

The division of Korea at the 38th parallel in the aftermath of World War II laid the foundation for future conflict. The Soviet Union occupied the northern part of the peninsula, while the United States occupied the south. The ideological divide between communist and non-communist forces foreshadowed the tensions that would erupt into open warfare.

2. Outbreak of War: North Korean Invasion

In June 1950, North Korean forces, led by Kim Il-sung, launched a surprise invasion of South Korea, seeking to reunify the peninsula under communist rule. The sudden aggression caught the international community off guard and prompted a swift response from the United Nations, which called for collective action to repel the North Korean invasion.

3. International Involvement: A Global Conflict

The Korean War evolved into an international conflict, with nations aligned along Cold War lines joining the fray. The United States, along with a coalition of United Nations forces, intervened to support South Korea, while China and the Soviet Union backed the North. The war became a proxy battleground in the larger geopolitical struggle between East and West.

4. Stalemate at the 38th Parallel: A Brutal Conflict

The Korean War was marked by intense fighting, including the Battle of Inchon and the Chosin Reservoir campaign. However, by 1951, the conflict reached a stalemate along the 38th parallel. The war became a protracted struggle of attrition, characterized by trench warfare reminiscent of World War I. The human toll was staggering, with millions of soldiers and civilians caught in the crossfire.

5. Armistice and Unresolved Tensions: Legacy of the Korean War

In 1953, an armistice agreement was signed, effectively ending the active fighting in the Korean War. However, no formal peace treaty was ever established, leaving the Korean Peninsula technically in a state of war to this day. The armistice created the demilitarized zone (DMZ) along the 38th parallel, solidifying the division between North and South Korea.

Legacy and Reconciliation: A Divided Nation

The Korean War's legacy is profound and enduring. The division of Korea remains a geopolitical fault line, and the demilitarized zone stands as a poignant symbol of unresolved tensions. The war is often referred to as the "Forgotten War," as its complexities and the lack of a clear resolution have relegated it to the periphery of collective memory. However, its impact on the geopolitical dynamics of East Asia and the lasting division of the Korean Peninsula continue to shape regional affairs.

Reflection: Remembering the Forgotten

As we revisit the Korean War, it is imperative to confront the complexities and consequences of this often overlooked conflict. The "Forgotten War" may not have the same prominence as World War II, but its influence on the geopolitics of the Korean Peninsula and the broader Cold War era cannot be understated. To remember the Korean War is to acknowledge the sacrifices of those who fought, the lasting scars on a divided nation, and the ongoing quest for reconciliation on a peninsula that remains at the crossroads of global tensions.

12.

Laos and Cambodia: The Secret Wars in Southeast Asia

In the turbulent years of the Cold War, Southeast Asia became a covert battleground where geopolitical rivalries played out in the shadows. The neighboring nations of Laos and Cambodia found themselves unwittingly thrust into the midst of these clandestine conflicts, as the United States, the Soviet Union, and their respective allies vied for influence. The secret wars in Laos and Cambodia, though overshadowed by the larger conflicts of the era, left an indelible mark on the region's history.

1. The Pathet Lao and the Ho Chi Minh Trail: Laos Becomes a Theater of War

In Laos, the communist Pathet Lao sought to establish control, drawing the attention of the United States. As part of the wider effort to disrupt North Vietnamese supply lines, Laos became a key battleground. The Ho Chi Minh Trail, a network of supply routes used by North Vietnamese forces, traversed Laos, making it a strategic target. The U.S. conducted covert operations, including the use of the Hmong people as allies, in an attempt to stem the flow of supplies to communist forces.

2. The Secret Bombing of Laos: Operation Rolling Thunder and Operation Arc Light

Laos bore witness to one of the most intensive and secret bombing campaigns in history. The U.S. launched Operation Rolling Thunder and later Operation Arc Light, dropping an estimated two million tons of bombs on Laos between 1964 and 1973. This covert bombing, aimed at disrupting North Vietnamese and Pathet Lao activities, had devastating consequences for the Laotian people, leaving a long-lasting impact on the country's landscape and population.

3. Cambodia and the Vietnam War: The Neutral Nation Drawn into the Conflict

Cambodia, officially neutral, became entangled in the Vietnam War as the conflict spilled across its borders. The North Vietnamese utilized the Ho Chi Minh Trail, which passed through eastern Cambodia, as a crucial supply route. In response, the U.S. initiated covert military operations within Cambodia, including the controversial and secret bombing campaign known as the "Operation Menu." These actions further destabilized the region and contributed to the rise of the Khmer Rouge.

4. Khmer Rouge and the Cambodian Genocide: Unintended Consequences

The secret bombings and covert operations in Cambodia unintentionally contributed to the destabilization of the nation. The Khmer Rouge, led by Pol Pot, seized power in 1975 and orchestrated a brutal genocide that resulted in the deaths of an estimated two million Cambodians. The unintended consequences of U.S. intervention and the secret wars cast a long and tragic shadow over Cambodia, shaping its history for decades to come.

5. Legacy and Reckoning: Coming to Terms with the Past

The secret wars in Laos and Cambodia left a complex legacy. The scars of the covert conflicts, including the unexploded ordnance in Laos and the trauma of the Cambodian genocide, continue to impact these nations. In recent years, efforts have been made to address the legacy of the secret wars, including demining initiatives and attempts to bring those responsible for war crimes to justice. However, the wounds of the past remain deep, and the process of reckoning with the hidden histories of Laos and Cambodia is ongoing.

Reflection: Unveiling the Hidden Chapters

As we revisit the secret wars in Laos and Cambodia, it is crucial to unveil the hidden chapters of history and acknowledge the human cost of covert conflicts. The impact of these secret wars extends far beyond the years of active intervention, shaping the geopolitical landscape, fueling regional tensions, and leaving a profound imprint on the collective memory of the Laotian and Cambodian people. To understand the hidden wars is to grapple with the complexities of Cold War geopolitics and the unintended consequences that continue to reverberate through Southeast Asia.

13.

Granada and Panama: Small Wars with Big Consequences

In the late 20th century, two seemingly small nations—Grenada and Panama—became the focal points of military interventions that had significant and lasting consequences. While these conflicts were labeled as "small wars," their impacts echoed far beyond their borders, shaping regional dynamics, U.S. foreign policy, and perceptions of military intervention.

1. Grenada: Operation Urgent Fury

In October 1983, the United States, alongside Caribbean allies, launched Operation Urgent Fury in Grenada. The intervention was sparked by concerns over the construction of an airstrip that was believed to be a military asset and the political instability following the execution of Prime Minister Maurice Bishop. The rapid military action resulted in the removal of Cuban and Soviet influence, the restoration of order, and the establishment of a pro-Western government. While the intervention was relatively brief, it marked a turning point in Cold War dynamics and showcased the U.S. commitment to preventing perceived threats in its backyard.

2. Panama: Operation Just Cause

In December 1989, the United States initiated Operation Just Cause in Panama, aiming to remove General Manuel Noriega from power.

Noriega, once a U.S. ally, had become involved in drug trafficking and was accused of election fraud. The military intervention aimed to protect American lives, restore democracy, and uphold the rule of law. The swift operation resulted in Noriega's capture and imprisonment, but it also raised questions about the justification for intervention and the broader implications of U.S. military actions in the region.

3. Regional Dynamics: Shifting Alliances and Cold War Realities

Both interventions in Grenada and Panama occurred against the backdrop of the Cold War's final years. The strategic considerations and geopolitical dynamics of the era played a significant role in shaping the decisions to intervene. The U.S. sought to counter perceived threats to its interests, prevent the spread of communism, and assert its influence in regions that were considered strategically vital.

4. Human Costs and Controversies: Unintended Consequences

While the military interventions achieved their immediate objectives, they were not without controversy and human costs. The loss of civilian lives, questions about the legality and justification of the actions, and concerns about the precedent set by unilateral military interventions raised ethical and diplomatic challenges. The interventions in Grenada and Panama underscored the complexities of balancing national interests with the principles of international law and sovereignty.

5. Legacy and Reflection: Lessons Learned

The small wars in Grenada and Panama had lasting consequences that reverberate to this day. The interventions demonstrated the potential for unilateral military action to achieve short-term objectives but also highlighted the need for careful consideration of long-term consequences and international perceptions. The legacy of these interventions influences how the United States and the international community approach military interventions, emphasizing the importance of strategic foresight and a nuanced understanding of regional dynamics.

Reflection: Navigating the Shadows of Intervention

As we reflect on the small wars in Grenada and Panama, it becomes clear that seemingly localized conflicts can have far-reaching implications. The interventions showcased the delicate balance between asserting national interests and respecting the sovereignty of other nations. Examining these interventions invites us to navigate the shadows of military action, learning from the complexities and unintended consequences that arise when powerful nations intervene in the affairs of smaller states.

14.

The Balkans: America's Role in the Yugoslav Wars

Amid the dissolution of Yugoslavia in the early 1990s, the Balkans witnessed a series of brutal conflicts that would become known as the Yugoslav Wars. The United States, along with the international community, became entangled in the complex web of ethnic tensions, territorial disputes, and humanitarian crises that unfolded in the heart of Europe. America's role in the Yugoslav Wars would shape its approach to intervention, diplomacy, and the post-Cold War order.

1. Breakup of Yugoslavia: Ethnic Strife and Political Fragmentation

The breakup of Yugoslavia, marked by the declarations of independence by Slovenia, Croatia, Macedonia, and Bosnia and Herzegovina, set the stage for a series of interconnected conflicts. Ethnic and religious tensions, long suppressed during the era of Tito's Yugoslavia, resurfaced with a vengeance, leading to widespread violence and displacement.

2. Bosnia and Herzegovina: The Challenge of Ethnic Cleansing

The Bosnian War (1992-1995) witnessed some of the most egregious atrocities, including ethnic cleansing campaigns and the siege of Sarajevo. The United States, initially hesitant to intervene, eventually took a more active role through diplomatic efforts and military intervention. The Dayton Agreement in 1995, brokered with American involvement, brought an end to the war and established the framework for the post-war Bosnian state.

3. Kosovo: NATO Intervention

In the late 1990s, tensions escalated in Kosovo, an autonomous province within Serbia. Reports of human rights abuses and ethnic cleansing by Serbian forces prompted NATO, led by the United States, to intervene militarily in 1999. Operation Allied Force aimed to halt the violence and protect Kosovar Albanians. The conflict ended with the withdrawal of Serbian forces and the establishment of a UN-administered Kosovo.

4. Challenges of Intervention: NATO's Role and Lessons Learned

The U.S. role in the Yugoslav Wars showcased the challenges of intervention in complex ethnic conflicts. NATO's involvement raised questions about the legitimacy of military action, the responsibility to protect civilians, and the delicate balance between sovereignty and humanitarian concerns. The lessons learned from the Balkans would influence subsequent international interventions and shape the evolving concept of humanitarian intervention.

5. Legacy and Unresolved Issues: The Balkans Today

The legacy of the Yugoslav Wars continues to shape the political and social landscape of the Balkans. While the conflicts officially ended in the late 1990s, the region grapples with the consequences of the wars, including ongoing political tensions, unresolved disputes, and the complexities of post-conflict reconstruction. The Dayton Agreement, while bringing an end to the Bosnian War, has also been criticized for institutionalizing ethnic divisions.

Reflection: Navigating the Post-Cold War World

America's role in the Yugoslav Wars marked a crucial chapter in the post-Cold War era, influencing the evolution of international relations and humanitarian intervention. As we reflect on this period, it prompts us to consider the challenges of navigating a world marked by ethnic strife, humanitarian crises, and the responsibilities of powerful nations in addressing conflicts that transcend borders. The Balkans serve as a poignant reminder of the complexities and enduring consequences of intervention in the pursuit of peace and stability.

15.

The War on Terror: Unfinished Battles and Ongoing Conflicts

The post-9/11 era ushered in a new chapter in global geopolitics with the declaration of the "War on Terror." The United States, in response to the devastating attacks on September 11, 2001, initiated a series of military interventions and counter-terrorism operations that reverberated across the world. However, a critical analysis reveals a complex narrative marked by America's use of misinformation, the consequences of labeling certain groups as "terrorists," and the enduring costs of a protracted global conflict.

1. Origins of the War on Terror: Shaping Public Perception

The War on Terror, declared by President George W. Bush, was framed as a response to the threat posed by Al-Qaeda and its leader, Osama bin Laden. The rhetoric used by the U.S. administration portrayed a stark dichotomy between the forces of good and evil, simplifying complex geopolitical realities. This narrative, while rallying international support, also laid the groundwork for the subsequent military engagements in Afghanistan and Iraq.

2. Afghanistan: The Quest for Bin Laden and Nation-Building Challenges

The invasion of Afghanistan in 2001 aimed at dismantling Al-Qaeda and removing the Taliban from power. While the initial military campaign achieved some objectives, the subsequent nation-building efforts faced significant challenges. The complex socio-political landscape, coupled with the persistence of extremist elements, underscored the limitations of military intervention in achieving long-term stability.

3. Iraq: WMDs and the Unraveling of a Nation

The invasion of Iraq in 2003, justified on the grounds of Saddam Hussein's alleged possession of weapons of mass destruction (WMDs), revealed a troubling aspect of misinformation. The absence of conclusive evidence of WMDs raised questions about the veracity of intelligence and the decision-making process that led to a full-scale military intervention. The aftermath witnessed sectarian violence, the rise of extremist groups, and a protracted conflict that exacerbated regional instability.

4. Consequences of Labeling: From War on Terror to the Global Battlefield

The broad categorization of groups and individuals as "terrorists" in the context of the War on Terror had far-reaching consequences. The use of this label, often applied without clear definitions or legal processes, contributed to a global battlefield where different actors were targeted, leading to a proliferation of conflicts and the loss of countless lives. The conflation of disparate groups under the umbrella of terrorism also obscured the underlying complexities of regional conflicts.

5. Unfinished Battles and Ongoing Conflicts: The Toll on America and the World

As the War on Terror unfolded, the human and financial costs became staggering. Millions of lives were lost, societies were upended, and the geopolitical landscape was reshaped. The consequences of misinformation, the erosion of civil liberties, and the unintended spread of violence posed profound challenges. The concept of a "war" on an abstract and elusive enemy proved to be a protracted and complex endeavor, with no clear endpoint in sight.

Reflection: Lessons Learned and Moving Forward

A critical analysis of the War on Terror prompts a reflection on the lessons learned and the imperative to reassess strategies in the pursuit of global security. The unintended consequences, both for America and the international community, highlight the need for nuanced approaches, a commitment to transparency, and a recognition of the complexities inherent in addressing the root causes of extremism. Moving forward, acknowledging the mistakes and missteps of the past becomes crucial for shaping a more just and sustainable global order.

16.
War in Afghanistan: The Graveyard of Empires Revisited

The conflict in Afghanistan, spanning over two decades, represents a complex and multifaceted chapter in modern history. As the United States engaged in what became its longest war, the intervention in Afghanistan was marked by a range of challenges, geopolitical complexities, and unintended consequences. A critical analysis reveals the impact of America's intervention, raising questions about the human cost, strategic decision-making, and the enduring legacy of a conflict in the so-called "Graveyard of Empires."

1. The Soviet-Afghan War: Historical Parallels and Lessons Ignored

The Soviet-Afghan War of the 1980s, often referred to as the "Graveyard of Empires," provided a cautionary tale that, unfortunately, went unheeded. The Afghan conflict had historically proven challenging for external powers, yet the lessons from the Soviet experience were not fully considered as the United States entered the region in the aftermath of the 9/11 attacks.

2. The Invasion of Afghanistan: Seeking Justice and Ousting the Taliban

The U.S. invasion of Afghanistan in 2001 had the primary objectives of dismantling Al-Qaeda and ousting the Taliban regime that had provided a safe haven for the terrorist organization. While the initial military campaign succeeded in toppling the Taliban, the subsequent nation-building efforts faced significant challenges, including the complexities of Afghan tribal politics, the resiliency of insurgent groups, and the lack of a clear exit strategy.

3. Nation-Building Challenges: The Illusion of Quick Success

The concept of nation-building in Afghanistan proved to be an ambitious and elusive goal. Despite initial successes, the complexities of Afghan society, tribal rivalries, and a resilient insurgency hampered efforts to establish a stable and self-sustaining government. The notion of a quick and efficient transition to a democratic state proved to be an illusion, contributing to the protracted nature of the conflict.

4. Unintended Consequences: Civilian Casualties and Humanitarian Costs

The War in Afghanistan exacted a heavy toll on civilians, with millions facing displacement, loss of life, and disruptions to daily life. The use of drone strikes, night raids, and other military tactics, while aimed at combating insurgency, resulted in unintended consequences. Civilian casualties fueled anti-American sentiments, contributing to the cycle of violence and making it difficult to win the hearts and minds of the Afghan population.

5. Strategic Shifts and the Dilemma of Withdrawal: Changing Priorities

As the conflict persisted, the shifting nature of global geopolitics and changing priorities led to strategic recalibrations. The announcement of a U.S. withdrawal raised questions about the long-term impact on Afghanistan's stability, the resurgence of insurgent groups, and the legacy of America's intervention. The question of whether the intervention achieved its original objectives or contributed to lasting positive change remained a subject of debate.

Reflection: The Imperative of Learning from Mistakes

A critical analysis of America's intervention in Afghanistan necessitates a candid reflection on the mistakes made, the human cost incurred, and the complexities of nation-building in a region with a tumultuous history. The "Graveyard of Empires" moniker serves as a stark reminder that military interventions, particularly in culturally intricate landscapes, demand nuanced approaches and an acute awareness of historical precedents. As the world reflects on the end of the War in Afghanistan, the imperative lies in learning from the mistakes of the past to inform more prudent and ethical decisions in the future.

17.

Iraq War: The Unraveling of a Nation

The Iraq War, initiated in 2003, stands as one of the most controversial military interventions in recent history. The unraveling of Iraq was marked by the pretext of Weapons of Mass Destruction (WMDs), a narrative that later proved to be a critical misrepresentation. A critical analysis of the Iraq War reveals the impact of the big lie about WMDs, the destruction wrought upon a once-beautiful nation, and the enduring consequences that continue to shape Iraq's trajectory.

1. The Big Lie: WMDs and the Justification for War

The central justification for the Iraq War was the claim that Saddam Hussein possessed Weapons of Mass Destruction. The narrative, championed by the Bush administration, provided the casus belli for military intervention. However, subsequent investigations and inspections failed to substantiate the existence of significant WMD stockpiles, revealing a critical misrepresentation that had far-reaching implications.

2. Shock and Awe: The Unleashing of Military Force

The military campaign, characterized by the doctrine of "Shock and Awe," unfolded with overwhelming force. While the initial stages of the invasion resulted in the rapid overthrow of Saddam Hussein's regime, the absence of a clear plan for the post-invasion phase contributed to a power vacuum, sectarian tensions, and the rise of insurgency.

3. Sectarian Unrest: The Unraveling of Iraq's Social Fabric

The aftermath of the Iraq War witnessed a profound unraveling of the nation's social fabric. Sectarian tensions between Sunni and Shia communities escalated, leading to cycles of violence and reprisals. The destruction of institutions, displacement of populations, and the erosion of social cohesion exacerbated Iraq's internal strife.

4. Insurgency and Rise of Extremism: Unintended Consequences

The vacuum created by the removal of Saddam Hussein's regime and the disbanding of the Iraqi army paved the way for insurgent groups, including Al-Qaeda in Iraq. The ensuing insurgency and the later emergence of the Islamic State (ISIS) highlighted the unintended consequences of military intervention, with extremist groups exploiting the power vacuum and capitalizing on the discontent fueled by the aftermath of war.

5. Humanitarian Toll and Destruction of Heritage: A Once-Beautiful Nation Scarred

The human toll of the Iraq War was staggering, with civilian casualties, displacement, and the destruction of infrastructure contributing to a protracted humanitarian crisis. Iraq, once a cradle of civilization with rich cultural heritage, witnessed the devastation of historical sites, artifacts, and monuments, further erasing the beauty that once defined the nation.

Reflection: Confronting the Legacy of the Iraq War

A critical analysis of the Iraq War compels a deep reflection on the decisions that led to military intervention, the human cost incurred, and the enduring consequences that continue to shape Iraq's present and future. The misrepresentation of WMDs, the lack of post-invasion planning, and the unintended escalation of violence underscore the need for careful consideration of the complexities involved in decisions of war and peace. As the international community grapples with the legacy of the Iraq War, it serves as a stark reminder of the imperative to learn from the mistakes of the past and approach geopolitical challenges with humility, foresight, and a commitment to the principles of justice and human dignity.

18.

African Interventions: From Somalia to Libya

The involvement of the United States in African interventions, spanning from Somalia to Libya, represents a complex tapestry of military engagements, humanitarian efforts, and geopolitical considerations. A critical analysis of America's role in these interventions reveals a range of challenges, ethical dilemmas, and the need for nuanced approaches in navigating the intricacies of African conflicts.

1. Somalia: Humanitarian Intentions and Unintended Consequences

The U.S. intervention in Somalia during the early 1990s, often referred to as Operation Restore Hope, initially aimed at addressing a humanitarian crisis. However, the mission faced challenges as the United States became entangled in local power dynamics and faced unexpected resistance. The Battle of Mogadishu in 1993, depicted in the film "Black Hawk Down," highlighted the complexities of military intervention in a complex and volatile environment.

2. Rwanda: A Tragic Omission and the Legacy of Inaction

The 1994 Rwandan genocide stands as a tragic chapter where the international community, including the United States, failed to intervene effectively. The absence of decisive action during the genocide raised questions about the responsibilities of powerful nations to prevent mass atrocities and the ethical implications of non-intervention.

3. Sudan and South Sudan: Balancing Diplomacy and Intervention

The United States has grappled with the ongoing conflicts in Sudan and South Sudan, where ethnic tensions, resource disputes, and governance challenges have fueled violence. American involvement has been marked by a balance between diplomatic efforts, peacekeeping initiatives, and considerations of military intervention, reflecting the complexities of navigating conflicts in the region.

4. Libya: The Arab Spring and Unintended Consequences

The intervention in Libya in 2011, part of the broader Arab Spring movements, aimed at protecting civilians from the Gaddafi regime's violent crackdown. However, the military intervention, authorized by the UN Security Council, led to the ousting of Gaddafi and the subsequent power vacuum, contributing to ongoing instability, civil strife, and the rise of extremist groups.

5. Counterterrorism in the Sahel: Regional Approaches and Challenges

The Sahel region has become a focal point for counterterrorism efforts, where the United States has supported regional partners in addressing threats posed by groups like Boko Haram and al-Qaeda in the Islamic Maghreb (AQIM). While cooperative efforts aim to enhance regional security, the challenges of governance, poverty, and complex regional dynamics persist, raising questions about the long-term effectiveness of military interventions.

Reflection on America's Role: Ethical Considerations and Strategic Pragmatism

A critical analysis of America's role in African interventions necessitates reflection on the ethical considerations and strategic pragmatism that shape decision-making. The balance between humanitarian objectives, regional stability, and the potential unintended consequences of military interventions underscores the need for a nuanced and context-specific approach.

Lessons Learned and Moving Forward: Toward Sustainable Solutions

As the United States continues to engage with African conflicts, the lessons learned from past interventions become crucial. Sustainable solutions require not only military considerations but also diplomatic, economic, and humanitarian approaches that address the root causes of conflicts. Acknowledging the limitations and unintended consequences of intervention is essential for shaping a more effective and ethically grounded approach to addressing the complex challenges facing the African continent.

19.

War on the Horizon: Emerging Threats and Future Challenges

As the global landscape evolves, the United States finds itself confronting emerging threats and challenges that strain its traditional role as the "global police." A critical examination reveals that America's extensive spending on wars and weapons has not only weakened its economic and diplomatic standing but has also failed to yield substantial political gains. Instead, the cost has been measured in the loss of millions of lives and a perceptible erosion of the once-held image of a benevolent global leader.

The Economic Toll: Draining Resources for Dubious Returns

The massive expenditure on wars and military capabilities, spanning various conflicts from the Middle East to Afghanistan, has imposed a significant economic burden on the United States. The trillions of dollars poured into military endeavors have not translated into proportionate political or economic advantages. Instead, these financial commitments have strained domestic resources, leading to budgetary challenges and hindering investments in critical areas such as education, infrastructure, and healthcare.

Diplomatic Fallout: Waning Soft Power and Eroding Alliances

The unrestrained pursuit of military solutions to global challenges has weakened the United States' soft power—the ability to influence through attraction and persuasion. As America became entangled in protracted conflicts with diminishing returns, its diplomatic capital waned. Erosion of alliances and strained international relationships further illustrates the diminishing efficacy of a militarized approach to global issues.

Human Costs: Millions Lost and Displaced in Pursuit of Hegemony

The toll in human lives has been staggering, with millions of casualties and displaced populations as a consequence of military interventions. The narrative of America as a global force for good has been tarnished by the unintended consequences of wars, fostering anti-American sentiments and contributing to a cycle of violence that undermines broader efforts for peace and stability.

Militarization at the Expense of Social Progress: Striking the Wrong Balance

The prioritization of military endeavors over domestic needs has skewed the balance between national security and societal well-being. The exorbitant costs of wars and military expenditures have diverted resources that could have otherwise been invested in education, healthcare, poverty alleviation, and infrastructure development. This misalignment jeopardizes the long-term strength and resilience of the nation.

A Shifting Global Image: The Decline of the Global Police Role

The perception of the United States as the "global police" has eroded as the limitations of military force in achieving lasting stability become increasingly apparent. The pursuit of unilateral military solutions has, at times, generated resentment and skepticism from the international community, challenging the notion of American exceptionalism and its role as a global arbiter of justice.

RETHINKING NATIONAL Security: Toward a Comprehensive Approach

As emerging threats, including cybersecurity, climate change, and global health crises, take center stage, a critical reassessment of national security priorities is imperative. A more comprehensive approach that integrates diplomatic, economic, and humanitarian strategies is essential. Redirecting resources toward addressing root causes and fostering international cooperation may prove more effective in securing America's interests and global stability.

7. A Call for Pragmatism and Reflection: Charting a New Course

The challenges on the horizon necessitate a pragmatic and reflective approach. It is time to acknowledge the limitations of a militarized foreign policy and to recalibrate national priorities. A more strategic and balanced approach that aligns with the evolving global landscape is crucial for safeguarding both the nation's well-being and its standing in the international community. The path forward requires wisdom, adaptability, and a commitment to a vision of global engagement that transcends the pitfalls of unilateral militarism.

20.

Reflections on Lost Wars: Lessons for the Future

As the echoes of lost wars reverberate through history, a moment of reflection becomes essential to distill the lessons that should shape the future trajectory of a nation. These reflections extend beyond the immediate political and military contexts, delving into the broader ramifications of failed endeavors. Each lost war holds within it valuable insights that, if heeded, can inform a more nuanced, strategic, and humane approach to navigating the complex challenges that lie ahead.

1. The Cost of Unbridled Ambition: Reassessing Global Roles

Lost wars underscore the perils of unbridled ambition and the potential pitfalls of striving for unchecked global dominance. The lessons gleaned call for a reassessment of the nation's role in the world, emphasizing collaboration over coercion and acknowledging the limitations of imposing unilateral solutions. A more measured and cooperative approach to international relations is imperative.

2. Human Toll and the Imperative of Diplomacy: Prioritizing Lives Over Hegemony

The human toll exacted by lost wars serves as a poignant reminder of the paramount importance of human lives. A commitment to diplomacy and conflict resolution must take precedence over military adventurism. Lessons from the past underscore that true strength lies not merely in military might but in the ability to navigate disputes through dialogue, understanding, and mutual respect.

3. The Erosion of Trust: Rebuilding International Relationships

Lost wars erode trust, both domestically and on the global stage. Rebuilding international relationships requires humility, accountability, and a sincere commitment to collaborative problem-solving. Recognizing the interconnectedness of the world and cultivating alliances based on shared values rather than dominance can foster a more stable and cooperative global community.

4. Shifting Priorities: Balancing Defense with Social Progress

The misallocation of resources in pursuit of military dominance at the expense of social progress is a recurrent theme in lost wars. A recalibration of national priorities is in order, emphasizing investments in education, healthcare, and social infrastructure. Striking a balance between defense capabilities and societal well-being is not only a strategic imperative but a moral imperative for the nation's long-term strength.

5. Learning from Mistakes: Embracing Adaptive Strategies

Reflections on lost wars call for a fundamental shift in how the nation learns from its mistakes. Embracing adaptive strategies involves a willingness to reassess and modify approaches based on evolving circumstances. It demands a departure from rigid ideologies and a commitment to agile, context-specific solutions that address the root causes of conflicts.

6. Redefining Leadership: Wisdom, Pragmatism, and Inclusivity

Leadership in the aftermath of lost wars necessitates a redefinition that embraces wisdom, pragmatism, and inclusivity. It requires leaders who prioritize the well-being of their people, acknowledge the complexity of global challenges, and champion collaboration over confrontation. True leadership emerges not from asserting dominance but from fostering a collective vision that uplifts all.

7. Cultivating a Legacy of Peace: A Vision for Future Generations

The ultimate lesson from lost wars is the imperative to cultivate a legacy of peace. This involves a commitment to resolving conflicts through dialogue, upholding human rights, and championing justice. As the nation reflects on its past, the vision for the future should be one in which succeeding generations inherit a world shaped by compassion, cooperation, and a profound understanding of the lessons that history imparts.

ABOUT THE AUTHOR

As an author deeply committed to fostering a vision of a peaceful future, I traverse the realms of history, politics, and international affairs with an unwavering belief in the power of words to inspire positive change. My hope is anchored in the prospect of a world unburdened by the shadows of America's terror wars, where the lessons from past conflicts serve as guideposts toward a more harmonious and just global community.

My writing reflects a commitment to dismantling the narratives of militarized dominance and advocating for a paradigm shift towards diplomacy, cooperation, and empathy. In exploring the untold chapters of history and dissecting the complexities of lost wars, I strive to illuminate the path toward a future where dialogue supersedes conflict, and collaboration replaces coercion.

The aspiration for a peaceful future is not merely a thematic thread in my work but a guiding principle that shapes my perspective on international relations. I believe in the transformative potential of acknowledging past mistakes, learning from them, and forging a collective commitment to building bridges rather than walls.

With a background rooted in a profound appreciation for the human experience and an unyielding dedication to peace, I invite readers to embark on a journey of reflection, understanding, and envisioning a world where the legacy we leave for future generations is one defined by compassion, justice, and the pursuit of a lasting and harmonious coexistence.

www.ingramcontent.com/pod-product-compliance
Lightning Source LLC
Chambersburg PA
CBHW061401140726
47997CB00003B/1311